GRAVITY

by Robin Nelson

first step nonfiction

Lerner Publications Company · Minneapolis

Gravity is a **force.**

A force is a push or a pull.

Gravity pulls things and
people to the ground.

Gravity pulls things down.

Gravity pulls leaves down.

Gravity pulls water down.

Gravity pulls apples down.

Gravity pulls a ball down.

Gravity pulls a roller
coaster down.

Gravity pulls a sled down.

Gravity pulls sand down.

Gravity pulls a **yo-yo** down.

Gravity pulls
sky divers down.

Gravity pulls rain down.

Gravity pulls me down.

Gravity is everywhere.

The Leaning Tower of Pisa

Galileo

Galileo

Long ago, a scientist named Galileo did an experiment with gravity. The story says that he went to the top of the Leaning Tower of Pisa and dropped two balls. One ball was heavy, and one was light. The two balls hit the ground at the same time. This showed that gravity pulls all objects to the ground at the same speed no matter what they weigh.

Gravity Facts

 Gravity pulls things toward the center of Earth.

 There is very little gravity in space. This is why astronauts float around in space.

 Your weight is the amount of force pulling you down to the ground.

 The Sun's gravity attracts the planets.

Earth's gravity draws the Moon toward Earth. Without it, the Moon would go flying into space.

 One story says that a scientist named Sir Isaac Newton first started thinking about gravity when an apple fell from a tree and hit him on the head.

Glossary

 force – a push or pull on an object

 gravity – a force that pulls things

 sky diver – someone who jumps from an airplane

 yo-yo – a toy that goes up and down on a string

Index

The photographs in this book are reproduced through the courtesy of: © Richard Cummins, cover, p. 10; Digital Vision Royalty Free, pp. 2, 22 (middle); Brand X Pictures, pp. 3, 22 (second from top); © Tom Stewart/CORBIS, p. 4; © Diane Meyer, p. 5; © Index Stock Imagery/David Davis, p. 6; © Brian Lawrence/SuperStock, p. 7; © Bonnie Sue, p. 8; PhotoDisc Royalty Free by Getty Images, pp. 9, 12, 14, 17, 22 (top and second from bottom); © Steven Graham Photography, p. 11; © Todd Strand/Independent Picture Service, pp. 13, 22 (bottom); © David Cavagnaro/ Visuals Unlimited, p.15; © Image Source Ltd., p. 16; Corbis Royalty Free, p. 18 (left); New York Public Library, p. 18 (right).

Lerner Publications Company
A division of Lerner Publishing Group
241 First Avenue North
Minneapolis, MN 55401 U.S.A.

Website address: www.lernerbooks.com

Library of Congress Cataloging-in-Publication Data

Nelson, Robin, 1971–
    Gravity / by Robin Nelson.
        p.   cm. — (First step nonfiction)
    Includes index.
    Summary: An introduction to gravity and its effects.
    ISBN: 0–8225–5133–0 (lib. bdg. : alk. paper)
    ISBN: 0–8225–5297–3 (pbk. : alk. paper)
    1. Gravity—Juvenile literature. [1. Gravity.] I. Title. II. Series.
QC178.N45 2004
531'.6—dc22   2003013884

Manufactured in the United States of America
1 2 3 4 5 6 – DP – 09 08 07 06 05 04

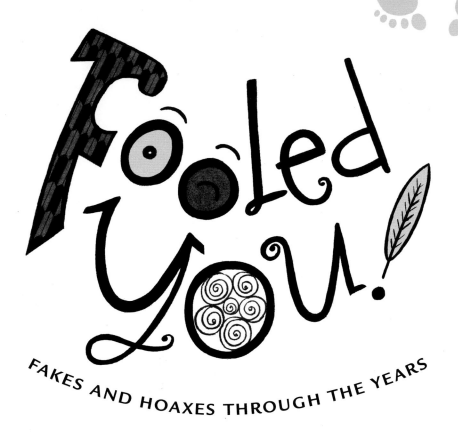

Fooled You!

FAKES AND HOAXES THROUGH THE YEARS

Elaine Pascoe

with illustrations by Laurie Keller

Henry Holt and Company · New York

Henry Holt and Company, LLC

Publishers since 1866

175 Fifth Avenue, New York, New York, 10010

www.HenryHoltKids.com

Library of Congress Cataloging-in-Publication Data

Pascoe, Elaine.

Fooled you! : fakes and hoaxes through the years /

Elaine Pascoe; with illustrations by Laurie Keller.—1st ed.

p.   cm.

Includes bibliographical references.

ISBN-13: 978-0-8050-7528-1

ISBN-10: 0-8050-7528-3

1. Impostors and imposture—Juvenile literature. I. Keller, Laurie, ill. II. Title.

CT9980.P37 2005   001.9'5—dc22   2004060732

First Edition—2005 / Printed in Mexico

3   5   7   9   10   8   6   4   2

To Fanny, good friend, who always tells the truth
—E. P.

Contents

Introduction

THIS IS TRUE—PLEASE TAKE THE TIME TO READ IT, AND PLEASE SEND THIS TO EVERY SINGLE PERSON YOU KNOW WHO HAS AN E-MAIL ADDRESS. . . .

If you use e-mail, you've probably received at least one message beginning like the above. Maybe it told you about Internet "cleanup day," when all Web servers are shut down for cleaning. Maybe it warned you of the death-ray virus, which can cause your computer to explode. Maybe it said that the U.S. Postal Service wants to charge a five-cent fee for every e-mail sent over the Internet.

And maybe you believed it. But you won't have to pay postage for sending e-mail, and there is no Internet cleanup day or death-ray virus. Those e-mails are hoaxes, made up just to trick people.

E-mail hoaxes are the latest twist in an old game. There have always been people who cooked up unbelievable tales—and other people willing to believe them. Many hoaxes are funny. Others have a darker nature; they're meant to ruin reputations or spread fear. Some are created to cheat people out of money. That's fraud, and it's a crime.

Hoaxes differ from practical jokes and other kinds of trickery, though. A practical joke is aimed at one person or, at most, a few people. Con artists who carry out frauds usually pick their victims carefully. But a hoax is meant to fool the world.

In this book you'll find the true stories behind some famous hoaxes. As you read them, ask yourself: Would I have been fooled?

CHAPTER ONE
The Daring Balloonists

On April 13, 1844, the *New York Sun* rushed out a broadside, a special edition, trumpeting a surprising story.

"Astounding News by Express, via Norfolk! The Atlantic Crossed in Three Days," read the headline. The report that followed was written by Edgar Allan Poe. It began:

> The great problem is at length solved! The air, as well as earth and the ocean, has been subdued by science, and will become a common and convenient highway for mankind. The Atlantic has actually been crossed in a Balloon!

A group of daring British adventurers, the account said, had made the amazing trip. Their leader was one Monck Mason, a well-known balloonist. Their craft was the "steering balloon *Victoria*," an egg-shaped, gas-filled balloon with a car hanging below it, something like a modern blimp. It had a spring-driven propeller and a rudder for steering.

The balloonists hadn't intended to cross the ocean, Poe's account revealed. They had meant to cross the English Channel from Britain to France. But the balloon's propeller broke, and a fierce northeast wind swept the craft out over the ocean. Traveling sixty miles an hour, and sometimes faster, the *Victoria* made the crossing in seventy-five hours. It landed safely on the coast of South Carolina.

The newspaper story included excerpts from a diary kept by Mason during the trip and a drawing of the *Victoria*. It caused quite a stir. As word of the news spread, people jammed the square in front of the *Sun* building, all eager to get a copy of the broadside. Enterprising newsboys made a profit by charging as much as fifty cents for a paper that usually sold for a penny.

Those who bought a copy thought they were holding a bit of history in their hands. Actually, they were being had.

Flight of Fact or Fancy?

Edgar Allan Poe is famous today as the author of short stories, such as "The Tell-Tale Heart." But he was not so famous in 1844. In fact, he was broke. In early April he arrived in New York from Philadelphia with five dollars in his pocket. He had a sick wife and a mother to care for, and he needed money quickly.

For a writer at that time, newspapers were the most likely source of quick cash. New York's three daily news-papers—the *Sun*, the *Herald*, and the *Tribune*—competed hotly for readers. Each wanted to be first with the next big story. And as Poe knew well, they did not always worry whether the stories they printed were true.

The *Sun* in particular was famous for this. In August 1835, for example, the *Sun* ran a series of articles claiming that a noted British astronomer had used a powerful new telescope to observe the moon. He had seen oceans, forests, animals, and—most amazing of

all—furry, bat-winged moon people! It was all fiction, of course. But in those days people knew little about conditions on the moon, and the stories were widely believed. The *Sun*'s circulation tripled before the hoax was exposed.

So Poe picked up his pen and wrote a story that the *Sun* couldn't pass up. Ballooning was a perfect topic—a balloon craze was sweeping the United States and Europe. Ballooning was the only way to fly, as airplanes hadn't yet been invented. It was new and exciting. People had been going up in hot-air and gas balloons for only about fifty years. Crowds turned out to watch balloon ascents, and daring balloonists tried to set new distance records. Crossing the Atlantic was the great ballooning dream. Just a year before Poe wrote his story, the American balloonist John Wise had described a plan

5

to ride a "current of air" across the ocean. He hadn't been able to raise money for the flight.

Poe made his story believable by including the names of real people. Monck Mason, for example, had actually sailed a balloon from London to Germany in 1836. Poe copied the drawing and description of the craft from a pamphlet that described similar balloons. The details made it easy for readers to accept that ballooning's

great goal had been reached. Neither they nor Poe knew that the east-to-west balloon crossing he described was all but impossible. The jet stream, the major upper-air current across the Atlantic, blows west to east. But the jet stream hadn't been discovered yet.

The *Sun* could have uncovered the hoax before printing the story. Its editors could have tried to contact Mason in South Carolina, where he supposedly had landed. They would have learned that the story was a fake. But in 1844 there were no telephones and no telegraph between New York and South Carolina. Checking the story would have taken days—and cost the *Sun* the chance to be first with the news.

It wasn't long before the truth came out, however. Two days after the story appeared, the newspaper admitted its mistake with a simple line: "The mails from the south . . . not having brought confirmation of the balloon from England . . . we are inclined to believe that the intelligence is erroneous."

No flying machine would cross the Atlantic until 1919, when a U.S. Navy seaplane made the trip. No balloon would cross until 1978, when the *Double Eagle II* sailed from Maine to France.

Today newspapers wouldn't be fooled by a made-up story like Poe's. Reporters and editors are supposed to check information, and they usually do. But every so often, they bend that rule. They rush to print an exciting story and only later discover that it was a hoax.

CHAPTER TWO

The Lost Princess

The young woman was clearly in distress. She had wandered into a village near Bristol, England, in April 1817, penniless and alone. She babbled words no one could understand. And she was strangely dressed, with a black shawl wrapped around her head like a turban. Who was she? Where had she come from? What did she want?

The villagers brought the stranger to the home of the local magistrate, Samuel Worrall, hoping he could solve the mystery. He could not, but his wife was fascinated. Determined to learn the story, she invited the woman to stay at their home.

The young stranger called herself Caraboo, and the Worralls found her customs as odd as her clothes. She preferred rice to bread and ate no meat. She drank only water and tea, always rinsing the cup before she drank. She prayed to a god she called Alla Tallah and washed her hands and face at every chance. She could shoot arrows and fence with a stick, which she carried in place of a sword. At times she carried a gong, which she

banged now and then, and wore flowers and feathers on her head. To the shock of polite society, she also climbed trees and, once, took off her clothes to swim in a lake.

Caraboo seemed to be delighted by anything from Asia—ivory fans, a Chinese puzzle, India ink, green tea, spices, a picture of a pineapple. Through gestures, she let it be known that these things were familiar to her from her homeland. Eventually an interpreter—a Portuguese sailor who claimed to know her language—turned up, and Caraboo's story came out. She was a princess from the island of Javasu, and pirates had kidnapped her. They had taken her to England, where she escaped by jumping overboard and swimming to shore.

For weeks Princess Caraboo captivated local society with her exotic dress and manners. Everyone wanted to meet her. Everyone tried to figure out where, exactly, Javasu was. Experts on Asia arrived to interview her. She was invited to the best homes. Artists painted her portrait. Newspapers printed stories and letters about her. Those reports were her undoing. Reading a description of Caraboo in the *Bath Chronicle*, a woman recognized

Tuzar
Puzar
Babalingoo
Pizzle Feezy
Doodle Geeble...
Loo
Lee
Loo
iddle
pooky!
ARRR!
Javasu...
kidnapped...
ARRR!
Overboard...
escaped...
Oh, dear!
Poor child!

the mystery princess as her former servant. The woman alerted Mrs. Worrall, who confronted her exotic guest. Caraboo, Princess of Javasu, confessed to being simple Mary Willcocks, of Devonshire.

Playing Princess

Mary Willcocks, who also went by the name Mary Baker, seems to have enjoyed playing "make-believe" and telling wild stories even as a child. She was the daughter of a cobbler, and her family was very poor. Like other poor women of her time, Mary had little education and few choices for making her way in the world. From the age of fifteen she had bounced from one servant position to another. Her employers all liked her—even if they thought she was more than a bit odd.

Mary had a hard life. At some point during her travels, she realized that acting like a foreigner could win help and sympathy from strangers. That was the start of her career as an impostor. But unlike many impostors, she didn't take on a false identity in order to get money or goods. She didn't ask for or take anything that wasn't freely offered by her hosts. She was treated

well as Princess Caraboo, and that was probably reason enough for her hoax.

The hoax succeeded largely because British people of the time knew little about other cultures. Trade between Britain and Asia was growing, and the British Empire was beginning to spread its rule over India and other parts of Asia. But most Britons had only vague notions of the way of life there. Caraboo's odd clothes and manners fit their picture of an Asian princess. So did the nonsense words that made up her "language"—words like *manjintoo* for "gentlemen" and *tuzar* for "ship."

In addition, people of the time were very conscious of class and were dazzled by rank. For someone like Mrs. Worrall, having a princess as a houseguest was the event of a lifetime. If there were flaws in Mary's performance, perhaps she didn't want to see them.

And Mary played her role well. From her arrival in April until June, when she was found out, she never let on that she spoke or understood a word of English. She listened closely as others talked about the places they thought she might have come from. She learned a lot about Asian customs from their talk, and she used what she learned to improve her performance as Caraboo.

She was also helped by the fact that she was pretty, charming, and likable. After her hoax was revealed, people still wanted to meet her and help her. The Worralls even paid her passage to America, where she spent seven years before returning to England.

Mary gave up trying to pass as a real princess after her hoax was discovered. But from time to time she dressed up as Caraboo and chattered away in her made-up language, just to entertain people.

CHAPTER THREE

The Fejee Mermaid

In the summer of 1842, New York City newspapers received a series of curious reports from the South. Writers from several cities wrote that Dr. J. Griffin, a British naturalist, had in his possession something truly amazing—an actual mermaid "taken among the Fegee Islands" in the Pacific Ocean. He was bringing the preserved specimen to New York on his way home to London from China, where he had bought it for the Lyceum of Natural History.

The newspapers jumped on the story, and curiosity began to build. Could the naturalist really have found a mermaid? The city would soon find out. Ads and flyers

appeared, announcing an exhibition. For "one week only," the public would have a chance to see a creature that had been known only through stories.

The mermaid was the talk of New York. People lined up to see it and to hear the scholarly Dr. Griffin speak about it. Most people had a bit of a shock when they actually laid eyes on the specimen, though. The Fejee Mermaid was not like the mermaids of fairy tales. Nor was it anything like the beautiful creatures pictured in the flyers advertising the exhibit. It was a small, dried, ugly thing—"the most odd of all oddities earth or the sea had ever produced," one newspaper wrote. Its upper body looked more like that of a monkey than a maiden.

Some people said it *was* a monkey's torso, joined to a fish's tail. But other people were sure it was real. There was no telltale seam between the body parts. And on display alongside the mermaid were specimens of other unlikely animals. There was a flying fish, for example, and a platypus—a mammal with a duck's bill and poisonous spurs on its rear legs. Naturalists had once thought the platypus was a hoax, but it turned out to be real. Perhaps the mermaid and the platypus were both what

the announcements for the exhibit claimed: "links in the great chain which connects the whole animal kingdom." After the weeklong exhibition, the Fejee Mermaid moved to the American Museum on Broadway. It drew crowds there for a month and went on tour to other cities. Everywhere the mermaid went, people paid to see it—whether they believed it was real or not. That was just what P. T. Barnum, the proprietor of the American Museum, had planned.

"People Love to Be Humbugged"

Phineas T. Barnum was probably the greatest showman in American history. In 1842 he had just bought the American Museum, which housed a dusty collection of oddities. He was determined to make it New York's leading attraction. And when he saw the Fejee Mermaid, he knew he had found a way to bring people through the museum's door.

The "mermaid" was just what it looked like—a dried monkey's body stitched to a dried fish's tail. Fake mermaids like this were nothing new. Sailors had been bringing similar curiosities back to America and Europe

for many years. This one had been around since 1817, when a sea captain bought it in the Pacific. Believing that it was real, the captain paid a small fortune for it. He never made money from his investment. After he

died, his family sold the mermaid to Moses Kimball, a Boston showman. Kimball leased it to Barnum for $12.50 a week.

How was Barnum able to turn this crude fake into an overnight sensation? With shameless hype. Barnum was a master at promotion. He didn't care whether people believed the mermaid was real or not. He knew that if he could create enough buzz about it, people would pay to see it.

The reports that appeared in New York newspapers were actually written by Barnum. He sent them to friends in Southern towns. The friends then mailed them to the New York papers over a period of weeks, in time with Dr. Griffin's supposed journey toward the city.

Griffin was no more real than the mermaid. The scholarly naturalist was actually Levi Lyman, a friend of Barnum's. He first took on the role in Philadelphia, where he allowed a small group of newspaper editors to have a peek at the mermaid. The stories they wrote helped build "mermaid fever" in New York. So did the flyers showing beautiful mermaids, which Barnum had printed.

Trumped-up science was part of the promotion, too. The first half of the 1800s saw a flowering of new theories and research in natural history. Barnum made his hoax more believable by having a "scientist" present it and by including actual animals such as the platypus in

the exhibit. Of course, real scientists were quick to spot the fake. But that didn't stop Barnum. New ads urged people to see the mermaid and draw their own conclusions. "Who is to decide when doctors disagree?" the ads declared.

The Fejee Mermaid helped make Barnum's museum a huge success. It was just one of countless curiosities that filled the museum's five floors. Like the mermaid, many of the exhibits were fake. No one seemed to mind. As Barnum said, "People love to be humbugged."

CHAPTER FOUR

The Stone Giant

On a crisp October day in 1869, two hired workers began digging a well on a farm in Cardiff, New York. Just three feet down in the soft ground, their shovels struck something hard. It was a stone, but a very strange stone: It was shaped like a huge human foot.

The men dug farther. The huge foot was attached to a huge leg. And the huge leg belonged to an enormous humanlike form—a ten-foot-tall stone giant, buried in the earth.

The workers rushed to tell the farmer who owned the land. The farmer rushed to tell his neighbors. And before long people for miles around were on their way

to the farm to gawk at the strange discovery. They came in droves, carried by special stagecoaches and filling local hotels. The farmer, Stub Newell, put a tent over the excavation site and charged admission. At fifty cents a head, he made good money.

Many of the tourists were certain that this was an actual giant that had turned to stone, or petrified. They had heard tales about petrified men, and the Book of Genesis in the Bible spoke of "giants in the earth." This giant looked real enough, right down to the pores in his skin. Shadowy blue lines revealed his veins. His body was slightly twisted, with his right hand clutching his stomach, as if he had died in great pain.

Several scientists, including New York's state geologist, came up with a different explanation. There was no evidence that flesh could turn to stone, they said. The giant was probably an ancient statue, carved by Native Americans long ago. It was covered with stains and marks of erosion, clear signs that it had been in the ground a long time.

Even people who were skeptical wanted to see this amazing discovery. Expecting to turn a handsome

profit, a group of investors paid $30,000 for two-thirds ownership of the Cardiff Giant. They put their treasure on display in Syracuse, New York, in November. A special railroad stop was set up to handle the expected crowds.

But by then doubts were growing. A famous scientist from Yale University saw the giant and pronounced it fake—a "decided humbug of recent origin." Reporters began to dig into the story of the statue's discovery. Locals remembered a large crate that was shipped to the Newell farm a year earlier.

By early December, the man behind the Cardiff Giant had come forward with the truth.

A Giant of a Hoax

George Hull, Stub Newell's brother-in-law, was the man who dreamed up the Cardiff Giant. A cigar maker from Binghamton, New York, Hull got the idea for the hoax in 1868, after arguing with a preacher who insisted that there really were giants in biblical times. He decided to play a joke on the preacher and others who took the

Bible literally—and maybe make some money at the same time.

Hull ordered a huge block of gypsum, a soft stone, and had it shipped to a stonecutter in Chicago. The stonecutter carved the giant to Hull's order.

The result was incredibly detailed. Natural blue veins in the stone looked like human veins. Pores were put on by hammering the surface with a mallet faced with darning needles. A final dip in acid gave the figure an aged look.

Hull put the giant in a crate, shipped it to upstate New York, and delivered it to Newell's farm in November 1868. He and Newell buried it there and left it in the ground for nearly a year. Then, on Hull's instruction, Newell hired the well diggers and told them where to dig. He knew very well what they would find.

When the giant was unearthed, a lot of people were ready to believe it was real. This part of New York had been the scene of many feverish religious revivals—so much so that it was called the Burnt-Over District. It had more than its share of cults and sects, including many that took a literal view of the Bible. If the scriptures said there were giants in the earth, these people reasoned, one was bound to turn up sooner or later.

Besides, the giant was not the first oddity to be discovered in the area. Just a few months earlier, dinosaur bones had been found on a nearby farm. And back in 1827, in nearby Palmyra, a man named Joseph Smith claimed to have discovered golden plates that carried a divine text. Smith translated the text, the Book of Mormon, and founded the Church of Jesus Christ of Latter-day Saints.

Even after Hull admitted the hoax, people wanted to see the Cardiff Giant. In fact, the statue went on a national tour. Some people still insisted that the giant must be real, while others wanted to see if they would have been fooled.

The story of the Cardiff Giant has an odd twist. When the statue was put on display in Syracuse, P. T.

Barnum tried to buy it. His offer was turned down, but that didn't stop him. Barnum promptly had his own statue carved—a fake of a fake! He put it on display at his American Museum in New York City, claiming that

it was the "real" Cardiff Giant. It drew more visitors than the original.

No one today thinks the Cardiff Giant is real, but people are still paying to see it. The original statue is on view at the Farmers' Museum in Cooperstown, New York.

CHAPTER FIVE

The Marvelous Machine

The machine was a muddle of brass rods, wires, tanks, and gauges. But the businessmen who were invited to John Worrell Keely's Philadelphia workshop in 1874 were impressed. Keely poured some tap water into the machine and twiddled a few controls. Within minutes, a gauge showed pressure inside the machine rising to 10,000 pounds per square inch—proof, Keely said, that his device could turn out amazing amounts of energy.

How did it work? Keely explained: He had found a way to dissolve water and release the mysterious force of "luminiferous ether." The businessmen nodded. They had heard of the ether. Many scientists of the time

thought outer space was filled with this invisible vapor. So far no one had been able to capture or measure it. But if Keely's generator was as good as it seemed, it could be the start of something big.

The inventor just needed to develop a practical motor based on his discovery. Then a quart of water would be enough to send a train across the United States and back. A gallon would power a steamship round-trip between New York and England. Anyone who had a stake in this new source of energy was sure to make a fortune. The Philadelphia businessmen lined up to buy

shares in the new Keely Motor Company, and so did many other people.

Keely went to work on his motor. From time to time he staged demonstrations for his investors, awing them with scientific terms. He showed off such devices as a "hydro-pneumatic pulsating vacuo-engine" and a "vibratory accumulator." He used tuning forks or musical instruments to set off "sympathetic vibrations" that released the "etheric force." He showed how the force could break thick ropes, twist iron bars, and send bullets through foot-thick wood planks.

But a practical motor was slow in coming. Doubts grew. People began to listen to skeptics who said that Keely's theories were nonsense. By 1881 no one wanted to buy Keely Motor shares.

Just as he was about to run out of money, Keely found a wealthy backer—Clara Bloomfield-Moore, the widow of a Philadelphia paper manufacturer. She not only gave him money but also worked hard to get his ideas accepted.

Thanks to her efforts, several top scientists and engineers came to Keely's workshop. Among them was the noted physicist W. Lascelles-Scott of England. He

went away convinced that Keely had made a great discovery. Others were doubtful. E. Alexander Scott, an electrical engineer, thought that Keely's mysterious force was nothing more than compressed air. Wires that seemed solid were actually thin hollow tubes carrying air to power Keely's machine, he suspected.

There was a simple way to settle the question: cut the wires. When Keely refused to do it, even Clara Bloomfield-Moore lost faith in him. It wasn't until his death in 1898 that the full story came out, however.

Nothing for Nothing

After Keely died, investors who had sunk money in his company went to his workshop and carried off some of his machines. Outside the workshop, though, none of the machines worked.

The secret was in the workshop itself. Engineer E. Alexander Scott discovered it. With newspaper reporters in tow, Scott ripped away false floors, walls, and ceilings. He found hidden belts leading to a silent water-driven motor and hidden pipes leading to a tank of compressed air in the basement.

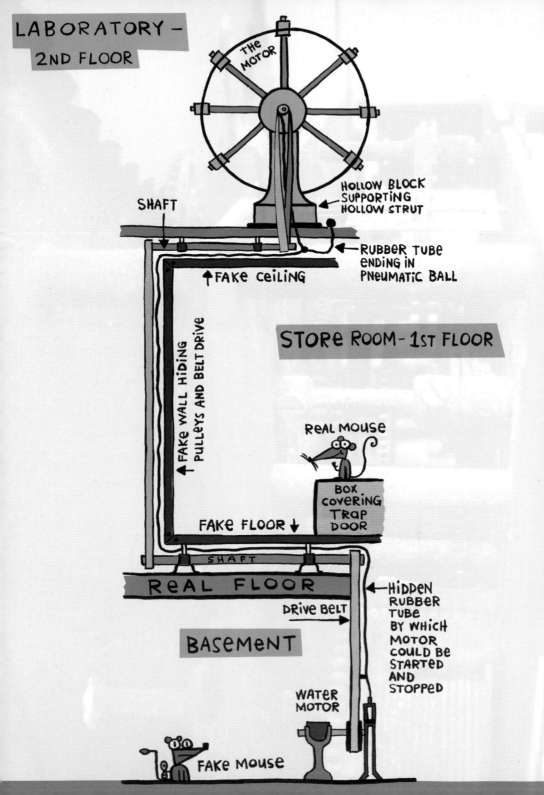

Keely's machines didn't generate energy at all. They *used* energy supplied by the water motor and compressed air.

Keely was not the first to come up with the idea of free energy. Since the Middle Ages, people had been trying to create "perpetual motion" machines—machines that would run forever, all on their own. These devices never worked. And from the mid-1800s on, scientists knew why.

The idea of free energy flew in the face of two basic laws of physics, the first and second laws of thermodynamics. (Thermodynamics is the study of how energy changes.) The first law says that energy can't be created or destroyed. It just changes form. For example, to produce electricity, a power plant burns coal or uses some other fuel. The plant releases the energy from the fuel and turns it into electricity.

The second law says that no system can turn out more energy than it takes in. When energy is converted from one form to another, some energy is always lost. The power plant produces less energy than it gets from the fuel it uses. In other words, you can't get something for nothing.

Since these laws were known in Keely's day, why did so many people fall for his hoax? Partly because the 1800s were a time of great change and growth in America. Industry boomed. Amazing inventions changed the way people lived. Electric motors, the telegraph, automobiles, and countless other inventions all appeared fifty years or less before Keely made his claims. Anything seemed possible.

Keely was not a scientist. He was a carpenter and a mechanic. But in his day inventing was almost a national pastime, and many inventors were self-made. Keely was a good talker, too. It wasn't hard for him to convince people that he had discovered the next big thing. Even scientists who should have known better were tempted by the idea of free energy.

The idea is still tempting. Today people use huge amounts of energy to light homes and offices and to power all kinds of machines, from cars to air conditioners. Much of that energy comes from burning coal, oil, and other fossil fuels. Cars and trucks run on gasoline. People use oil and natural gas to heat their homes. Power plants burn coal, oil, and natural gas to make electricity. These fuels pollute the air, and supplies of them are limited.

Every so often, someone announces a solution to the world's energy problems: an amazing device that creates more energy than it uses. Like Keely, these inventors cloak their claims in big words—theories of "gyroscopic particles" and "zero-point energy." So far no such device has worked, and it's not likely that one ever will.

CHAPTER SIX

The Missing Link

Arthur Smith Woodward, curator of geology at the British Museum, could hardly contain his excitement. There, on the table in front of him, were fragments of a fossil skull that might hold the key to the secrets of human evolution.

The year was 1912, a thrilling time for scientists. Fossils of early humans had been discovered in Asia and continental Europe. They seemed to support the revolutionary idea that humans had descended from apes—an idea put forward by Charles Darwin in 1871, in *The Descent of Man.* But the line of descent wasn't clear.

There were fossils of ancient apelike beings, with sloping foreheads and weak jaws. There were fossils of early humans, with high foreheads and strong jaws like those of modern people. There was nothing in between. Scientists everywhere were searching for evidence of the "missing link" between apes and humans.

And now Woodward had the evidence. Charles Dawson, a lawyer and an amateur archaeologist who often collected fossils for the museum, had brought the skull fragments to him. Dawson had discovered the bones at the Piltdown gravel quarry in southern England.

Woodward and Dawson returned to the quarry. Combing through the gravel, they turned up more exciting finds—a jawbone containing two teeth, and prehistoric tools of stone and bone. Nearby were the bones of several extinct prehistoric animals. If the skull and jaw dated to the time of these animals, the two men reasoned, the fossils were at least five hundred thousand years old.

The discovery caused a stir in the scientific world. A new member was added to the human family tree: *Eoanthropus* ("dawn man") *dawsoni* (for Dawson, the

discoverer). Most people just called the new find Pilt-down Man.

Piltdown Man had just the sort of mixed features expected in the "missing link"—skull bones like those of a human and a jawbone like that of an ape. British scientists were delighted that what seemed to be the ancestor of modern humans had turned up in their homeland. At first other scientists were not so sure. The jawbone and the skull, they said, might be from two different creatures. But then more fossils were found in the quarry—a tooth, and then a second skull. That convinced most people that Piltdown Man was real.

Still, it was hard to see where the fossils from the gravel quarry fit in the grand scheme of human evolution. And as time went on, it became harder. More fossils of human ancestors turned up in Asia, Africa, and other parts of the world. None resembled Piltdown Man. Their skulls were far more apelike, and their jaws more humanlike.

In 1949, scientists decided to test the Piltdown fossils with a new chemical dating method. This test measured the amount of the chemical fluorine in the bones. Buried bones absorb fluorine from the soil, and the amount absorbed increases with time.

To everyone's shock, the test showed that the Piltdown fossils were nowhere near five hundred thousand years old. They were much too young to be those of the "missing link." But what were they?

Fossil Fakery

In 1953, three British scientists—J. S. Weiner, Sir Kenneth Oakley, and Sir Wilfrid Le Gros Clark—examined the Piltdown fossils and put them through more tests. Their

findings made headlines: Piltdown Man was a complete fake.

The jawbone? It came from an ape, probably an orangutan. It had been treated with chemicals to appear ancient. The teeth? Also from an ape, and filed to seem more humanlike. The skull fragments? They were human and much older than the jaw, but nowhere near as old as had been believed. The prehistoric tools? Also fakes. The fossils of extinct animals? All, Weiner wrote, "were planted in the Piltdown gravel, in order to suggest that the skull was that of a man living before the Ice Age."

That was the end of Piltdown Man—and the beginning of a

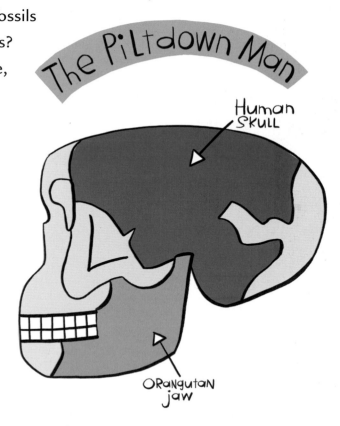

The Piltdown Man

Human Skull

Orangutan jaw

45

great mystery. Who made the fake fossils? To this day, no one knows.

Dawson, who died in 1916, had been first to search the Piltdown quarry. He had made the key finds on his own. He easily could have planted the fakes. He was the obvious suspect—but not the only one.

Woodward gained most from Piltdown Man. As the co-discoverer, he became famous. And some of his actions were hard to explain. He overlooked clear signs of fakery, like file marks on the fossil teeth. He didn't give other scientists a chance to study the fossils in detail. Woodward had an outstanding reputation. Many people didn't think he would have carried out the hoax.

Martin A. C. Hinton, a curator of zoology at the British Museum at the time, loved practical jokes and hinted to friends that the Piltdown finds might be fakes. In the 1970s a trunk bearing Hinton's initials was found in a loft at the museum. In it were stained bones, a lot like the Piltdown bones. But so far as anyone knows, Hinton wasn't at the quarry to plant fake fossils.

Others have been suspected, too. Whoever carried it out, the hoax fooled the world. It succeeded mainly

because, in 1912, scientists didn't have the tools and tests needed to unmask the fakes. They knew little about early human ancestors, and the Piltdown bones fit their expectations.

Today scientists have a different theory of human evolution. They believe that apes and humans shared a distant early ancestor, but they no longer think that modern people descended directly from apes. Thus there is no "missing link" between them.

CHAPTER SEVEN

The Fraudulent Fairies

Elsie Wright and her cousin Frances Griffiths burst into the Wrights' house and blurted out the most amazing news: They had met fairies along a stream near the house! Ten-year-old Frances had fallen into the water in her excitement.

It was the summer of 1917, and Frances and her mother were visiting the Wrights in the village of Cottingley, England. Not surprisingly, the adults in the house didn't believe the girls' fairy tale for a minute. But then Elsie, who was sixteen and knew a bit about photography, asked to borrow her father's camera to prove

their claim. To everyone's surprise, the girls later produced pictures that showed them surrounded by tiny fairies and gnomes.

The amazing pictures became the talk of the sleepy village, and word of them spread beyond. One of those who heard about them was Sir Arthur Conan Doyle, author of the Sherlock Holmes detective stories. Sherlock Holmes was famous for solving crimes through keen observation and logical reasoning. You might think the inventor of such a smart detective would be quick to dismiss the photos as fakes. But Doyle believed that fairies and other spirit beings might exist. When he saw the photos, he was convinced that they were genuine. In 1920, he asked the girls to take more pictures of their fairy friends, and they did.

The pictures, Doyle believed, proved that fairies existed. He wrote about them in magazine articles and in a book called *The Coming of the Fairies*. This caused quite a stir. While some people mocked him, others said he was right. It did not bother Doyle's supporters that no one but Elsie and Frances could see the fairies. The fairies were probably shy and might show themselves

only to children. Nor did it matter that the fairies in the
pictures seemed oddly flat and stiff. The camera couldn't
lie. Here was proof that fairies were real.

Sherlock Holmes would have known better.

A Little Fib Starts a Big Hoax

It all began when Elsie and Frances were late for lunch. Worse, Frances's clothes were soaking wet. She had been scolded before for falling in the stream. Now she would be scolded again—unless she had a good excuse. Put on the spot, the girls cooked up a story about fairies.

Perhaps the girls didn't really expect anyone to buy their tale. But when the adults scoffed at it, Elsie thought they would have some fun trying to prove it. Elsie was a talented artist and had worked for several months as a photographer's assistant. She copied pictures from a book to make cardboard cutouts of fairies, which the girls propped up with hatpins in the bushes along the stream. Then she took pictures with the borrowed camera.

When Elsie's father saw the photos, he figured that she was up to a prank. He took the camera away. But Frances's mother wasn't so sure. Photography was still fairly new in 1917, and like many people, she didn't know much about it. Perhaps the camera could see what the human eye could not. Perhaps there really

were fairies by the stream. She mentioned the pictures to friends who were interested in a movement called spiritualism.

Spiritualism, an odd blend of science and superstition, had spread throughout the United States and Europe beginning in the late 1800s. Scientific knowledge was growing at that time, but old folk beliefs did not die easily. Spiritualists searched for scientific evidence of spirits and other strange beings. They held gatherings called séances, at which they tried to contact the spirit

world by sitting together, holding hands, and listening for knocking sounds or other signs that spirits were present. Some even sat for "spirit photographs," in which ghostly images mysteriously appeared hovering behind them. The spirit photographs were double exposures, made by dishonest photographers. But spiritualists believed they were real.

Doyle was one such spiritualist. He was obsessed with the spirit world. Thus it was easy for him to accept that there might be photographs of fairies. He also didn't think that two "innocent" children would be able to fake the pictures. He wanted to believe, so he overlooked the fact that Elsie was skilled in art and in photography.

After Doyle wrote about the fairy photographs, Elsie and Frances became famous. They were much too embarrassed to admit that the whole affair had started with a fib. They kept their secret until 1983, when they finally explained how they had made the pictures. Even before then most people had realized that the photos weren't genuine. By today's standards, they are obvious fakes that wouldn't fool anyone.

CHAPTER EIGHT
The Brass Plate

In 1936, a young man walking near the shore of San Francisco Bay came across a dingy, battered sheet of metal. There was writing on the surface, and he could just make out the letters D-R-A-K-E. Curious, he took the metal plate to the University of California at Berkeley. There one of the state's leading historians, Herbert E. Bolton, examined it carefully—and declared it an amazing historical discovery. The plate, Professor Bolton said, was a brass marker that had been left on the California shore in 1579 by the English explorer Sir Francis Drake.

Drake was a privateer—a sort of legal pirate—who preyed on Spanish ships with the blessing of Queen Elizabeth I of England. In his day, England and Spain were bitter rivals. The Spanish feared Drake and called him El Draque, "The Dragon." But to the English, he was a hero—especially after he became the first Englishman to sail around the globe, from 1577 to 1580.

It was on that trip that Drake left the marker. He stopped at a sheltered bay somewhere on the California coast in June 1579 and stayed about a month to rest and repair his ship, the *Golden Hind.* Before leaving to

head across the Pacific Ocean, according to accounts of the time, he put up a brass plate, "nailed upon a fair great post." The marker claimed the country for England and named it Nova Albion (Latin for New England).

Drake returned to England with a fortune in looted Spanish gold and jewels. Queen Elizabeth promptly knighted him. But despite Drake's claim, California became Spanish territory. Spain and then Mexico controlled California until 1848, when the United States annexed it.

As English speakers, U.S. historians were naturally interested in the link between California and the English explorer. They tried to figure out exactly where in California Drake had landed. Scanning old accounts of the voyage for clues, they came across the description of the plate. What had become of it? Why had it never been found?

Professor Bolton was especially fascinated by stories of Drake's plate. He believed Drake had stopped near Point Reyes, a wild area north of San Francisco. The plate, he figured, should be somewhere in that area. He told his students to be on the lookout for it. And he was thrilled when the plate turned up. The brass was dark

and the letters were worn, but it matched the descriptions in the old accounts of Drake's voyage.

Historians hailed the discovery. The plate was placed in the collection of the Bancroft Library at Berkeley. Textbooks showed pictures of it. It was proudly displayed at the 1939 Golden Gate International Exposition in San Francisco as California's greatest historical treasure. In fact, it was California's greatest historical hoax.

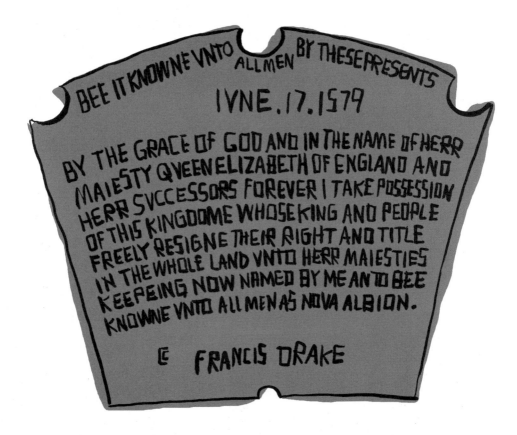

A Prank Out of Control

The plate was fake. That much became clear in 1977, when tests showed that the brass was milled in the twentieth century. The full story didn't come out until 2003. In that year, *California History* magazine ran an article by a team of historians who had spent eleven years researching the hoax.

It had begun as a simple prank among members of a historians' group named E. Clampus Vitus. The Clampers, as they were called, were known for practical jokes. Bolton was a Clamper, and his fascination with Drake's plate was well known. G. Ezra Dane, another Clamper, decided to trick him.

Four other men helped Dane. Together they designed the plate and carved the text. Then they heated the metal over a fire, hammered it, and rubbed it with dirt and ashes to darken the brass. On the back, they added the initials ECV in paint that would show up only in black light, to label the plate as a Clamper prank. They buried the plate for a while to "age" it and then left it on Point Reyes.

Their plan was to take Bolton on a hike and watch as he "discovered" the phony plate. Later, perhaps over a good dinner, they'd put it under black light and share a laugh with him. But before they could bring Bolton to the site, the plate disappeared.

The plate was carried off by William Caldera, a chauffeur who had driven his employer out to Point Reyes. Killing time while his employer hunted quail, Caldera came across the carefully planted fake. He stuffed it in the trunk of his car. But his interest soon faded. A few weeks later, he tossed it out along the shoreline road where it was later found.

To Bolton, the plate was the high point of his career. He had hoped to find it for so long, and he wanted it to be real. That's probably why he didn't see that it was a fake. He was a respected historian, so when he said that Drake's plate had been found at last, others took his word for it.

Dane and the other pranksters were dismayed. They had planned a private joke. None of them wanted to make Bolton seem foolish in front of the entire world. So instead of confessing the hoax, they just hinted to

Bolton that he should look more closely at his discovery. He didn't take their hints.

Bolton died in 1953, still sure that he had found Drake's plate. To this day, historians don't know exactly where Drake landed or what became of the real plate.

CHAPTER NINE

The Creature in the Woods

One morning in 1958, a worker carving a logging road through a forest in northern California returned to the clearing where he had parked his bulldozer the night before. All around the machine were strange footprints, unlike any he had ever seen. The tracks were humanlike, yet not human. Whatever had made them certainly had big feet—the prints measured sixteen inches, toe to heel.

A local newspaper ran a story about the strange discovery, calling the mystery animal "Bigfoot." The report sparked a buzz of interest. Was some sort of giant ape out there in the woods? Skeptics dismissed the idea. But a few people recalled Native American legends about

Sasquatch, a giant "man-creature" that haunted the ancient forests and mountains of the Pacific Northwest. And there had been reports of giant apelike creatures elsewhere—the Abominable Snowman, or Yeti, of Asia, for example.

Before long, other tracks were found, and there were more reports of Bigfoot. Some people said they had caught a fleeting glimpse of a hairy creature that stood between seven and ten feet tall. Others heard its bone-chilling howls or caught its scent—something like

a skunk, they said, but worse. And some just sensed its awful presence.

"Suddenly, I had this very bad feeling," a prospector reported. "I went down on my knees and covered my face and eyes with both hands and tried to hide. At that moment I heard an animal on two legs come down the trail. . . . I didn't look until after it left."

Far from being afraid of Bigfoot, some people went looking for the hairy beast. Two who did were Roger Patterson and Bob Gimlin. In October 1967, they filmed what seemed to be a female Bigfoot crossing a gravel streambed in Six Rivers National Forest, near the site where footprints had been found nine years earlier. The film convinced many people that Bigfoot was real. In 1969, one county in Oregon even adopted a law against killing what officials there called a "nocturnal primate mammal."

Several scientists jumped on the Bigfoot band-wagon, too. Grover S. Krantz, an anthropologist at Washington State University, was one. He argued that the creature was really a giant prehistoric ape, *Giganto-pithecus*, long thought to be extinct. Krantz analyzed the 1967 film frame by frame and studied casts of

footprints and other evidence. He concluded that there might be as many as two thousand of the giant apes prowling the wilds of the Pacific Northwest, feeding on roots and berries.

Krantz wasn't able to convince many other scientists, though. If thousands of giant apes were out there in the woods, most asked, why had no bones or other remains ever been found?

Bigfoot or Big Fake?

The mysterious creature who left footprints at Six Rivers in 1958 wasn't a giant ape. It was the bulldozer operator's boss, a logger and road-builder named Ray Wallace. At least, that's the story that came out after Wallace's death in 2002.

Wallace loved practical jokes. According to his family, he decided to play a trick on his worker. He had a friend carve a pair of sixteen-inch-long feet from wood, and he used them to make prints around the bulldozer, where he knew the worker would find them.

"It was just a joke, and then it took on such a life of its own that even now, we can't stop it," Michael

Wallace, one of Ray's sons, told a reporter. Ray Wallace kept quiet about the hoax and continued to milk it for the rest of his life, faking photos, footprints, and even recordings of Bigfoot sounds.

Wallace didn't produce all the evidence of Bigfoot, of course. Reports of the giant creature have come from all over the Northwest. But a lot of the reports have been questioned. Even the 1967 film is suspect. Does it show Bigfoot or someone in an ape suit? If you look closely, some people say, you can see a fastener amid the fur. And who sent the filmmakers to the streambed site? Ray Wallace.

People who have reported Bigfoot encounters aren't necessarily making up stories. But they've probably seen or heard something else. Perhaps they've caught a glimpse of a bear or heard the scream of a mountain lion. The power of suggestion can be very strong. If hikers think Bigfoot is in the woods, they may see the creature where it's not.

Reminders of Bigfoot are everywhere in parts of the Northwest, too. In the Six Rivers area, tourists drive the Bigfoot Scenic Byway, lunch on Bigfoot Burgers (shaped like big feet), and stay at the Bigfoot Motel. Bigfoot is a

big draw—and local businesses work hard to keep the stories alive.

Luckily for them, there are still plenty of people who are convinced that Bigfoot is real. The sightings and footprints can't all be faked, believers insist. Even some well-known scientists say the existence of a giant primate can't be ruled out.

But until someone captures a Bigfoot or finds the remains of one, most scientists won't be convinced.

CHAPTER TEN

The Sign in the Field

A strange sight greeted drivers on an English country road one morning in 1980. There, in a green hollow known as the Devil's Punchbowl, a mysterious sign had appeared in a wheat field. Stalks of wheat were bent flat to the ground in the shape of a perfect circle more than fifty feet across.

Drivers hit the brakes, stopped, and stared. News reporters hurried to the site. Within twenty-four hours, the mysterious circle was the talk of England. Swarms of tourists began to arrive, shattering the peace of the countryside.

Local farmers remembered seeing similar circles in the past. Who—or what—had made them, and why? If pranksters had been in the fields at night, they had left no footprints or other signs. Had swirling currents of air made the circles? Were crazed hedgehogs running in circles during their mating season? Were spaceships from distant planets landing in the fields? All those ideas were suggested.

Before long, other crop circles turned up. In fact, in the years that followed, hundreds of circles appeared in farm fields. England had the most, but there were sightings around the world. The circles all seemed to have been made the same way. The plant stems were rarely broken. They were just bent flat, in clockwise or counterclockwise spirals. Each year, the patterns of flattened stalks became more complex. There were circles within circles and circles joined by lines. There were arcs, triangles, keys, crosses, and rectangles.

Clearly, hedgehogs or wind currents couldn't form such complicated designs. And there were reports of strange goings-on when circles appeared. Dogs barked in the night. Some people saw mysterious lights or

heard warbling sounds. People who visited the circles claimed that they were filled with cosmic energy.

For some people, fascination with the circles developed into a field of study that they called "cerealogy." Cerealogists put forward several explanations for the events. Some said natural forces were at work. However, most claimed that visitors from another planet were making the circles as coded messages. None accepted the most likely explanation—that the circles were a hoax.

The Truth Is Out There—but the Hoax Is More Fun

A few years before the Devil's Punchbowl circle appeared, two men met at a pub near Winchester in southern England. Doug Bower and Dave Chorley, both watercolor painters, were old friends and regulars at the pub. On this warm summer night, they took their pints of ale outdoors. Looking over the fields, Doug remembered something funny that had happened years earlier, in his native Australia. When circles of flattened reeds had been found in a swamp there, some people had

claimed they were "UFO nests"—places where alien spaceships had landed.

Reports of UFOs (unidentified flying objects) had been common ever since 1947, when an American pilot claimed to have seen "flying saucers" over Washington State. Most reports were easily explained. People had mistaken weather balloons, meteors, or something else for alien spacecraft. Other reports were outright hoaxes. Still, many people took the reports seriously. After all, humans were beginning to explore space. Why couldn't intelligent beings from other planets be exploring Earth? By the 1970s, there were books, journals, and scholarly societies devoted to studying UFOs. And popular interest was fueled by dozens of science-fiction movies.

Fueled by their pints, Doug and Dave decided to create a few UFO nests of their own. They waited for darkness and then used a long iron bar to flatten a huge circle in a nearby wheat field. Over the next few years, they refined their technique, measuring out precise circles with a plank and a rope. But hardly anyone noticed the circles until they put one at Devil's Punchbowl, where it could be seen clearly from the road.

The two hoaxers had lots of laughs as "circlemania" broke out. Every time someone tried to explain the circles, they came up with new and more complicated patterns that defied the explanations. They finally confessed their prank to a newspaper reporter in 1991. By that time they had made at least two hundred crop circles. Copycat hoaxers, inspired by their work, made the rest.

You might think that would be the end of crop circles. But even after Doug and Dave demonstrated their circle-making techniques on television, many people refused to believe that aliens didn't make at least *some* of the circles. Nothing on Earth could have made the complex patterns, believers insisted. And what could explain the cosmic energy and mysterious lights and sounds?

In fact, there was no reliable evidence of cosmic energy and the other mysterious effects. There were only reports from individuals, and the reports often contradicted one another. But true believers just couldn't accept that they had been victims of a hoax. It was so much more exciting to think that aliens were trying to make contact. They wanted to believe.

Hoaxers have been happy to oblige. Doug and Dave are no longer out in the fields at night, but others are. Every year new circles and patterns appear in England and elsewhere. The hoaxers sit back and watch to see which ones the cerealogists will decide are "genuine."

CHAPTER ELEVEN

Snowball

You have mail—an e-mail message, forwarded by a friend:

Subject: You have to see this
Even if you are not a cat "person" you have to LOOK at
the picture!!!!!

The message tells how Rodger Degagne, an employee at a nuclear research lab in Chalk River, Ontario, Canada, discovered two stray kittens wandering near the facility. He took them home to his family. A few years later, the strays, now a full-grown male and female, had kittens of

their own. The Degagnes found homes for most of the kittens. They kept one, a white female with black markings. And that cat turned out to be something special, the message explains:

> Put simply, Snowball is no ordinary cat; she measures 69 inches from nose to tail and weighs in at 87 lbs. She started out a big kitty and she just seemed to keep growing.

Snowball swipes whole roast chickens off kitchen counters and sends German shepherds yelping for help. Instead of catching mice, she catches raccoons in the backyard. What made her grow so big? The message quotes her owner: "I think maybe her parents got into something at Chalk River that they shouldn't have."

In other words, Snowball is a giant nuclear mutant. Don't believe it? Just click to see the photo that's with the e-mail. There's Snowball, all eighty-seven pounds of her, in the arms of her proud owner.

When this e-mail message began to circulate in the spring of 2001, it made some people laugh. It made others wonder. Could it be true? Reporters and television

news crews scoured the Chalk River area in search of the monster cat. No one there knew anything about such an animal.

Internet Hoaxes

There was no giant mutant cat, of course. But the Snowball story shows why the Internet is a hoaxer's dream come true.

The cat in the e-mail picture was a perfectly normal house pet named Jumper. Jumper's owner, Cordell Haughlie, created the picture on his home computer. He combined a photo of himself with a close-up photo of his cat. Because of the difference in the scale of the two photos, Jumper looked supersized.

Haughlie didn't mean to start a hoax. He made the picture as a joke and sent it to his daughter. She forwarded it to friends, who forwarded it to other friends. Soon the photo was circulating on the Internet. At some point, someone—no one knows who—made up the Snowball story to go with the picture. From there the hoax . . . well . . . snowballed.

Internet hoaxes spread quickly because it's easy to forward e-mail messages to many people. One person starts the hoax in a message to ten people. Each of those people forwards it to ten more. By the time the message has been forwarded nine times, more than a billion e-mail messages have been sent!

Hundreds of such messages are flying around on the Internet all the time. They bring news of amazing deals— you can get a free trip to Disneyland just by forwarding the message to everyone you know. They spread false

warnings of deadly computer viruses and tell frightening stories about terrorists and street gangs. They urge you to send a sympathy card to a sick child somewhere.

Most people who start these e-mail hoaxes don't mean to do harm, but they still clog computer networks and interfere with regular e-mail. And like hoaxes of earlier days, some of these messages are intended to cheat people out of money. Some are meant to damage a person's or a company's reputation. And some, like false virus or terrorism warnings, cause a lot of unnecessary worry.

If you surf the Web, you'll find more hoaxes. Not long ago, for example, you might have come across the online diary, or Weblog, of Kaycee Nicole Swenson. This Kansas teenager wrote about

her experiences as a victim of leukemia, a type of cancer. Thousands of people followed her sad story online. They sent her encouraging messages, and some even sent her gifts. They were heartbroken when Kaycee's Web site finally announced her death. A few days later, the truth came out. Kaycee never existed. She was a fictional character created by Debbie Swenson, a forty-year-old homemaker in Peabody, Kansas.

Like Mary Willcocks, who dreamed up Princess Caraboo, Kaycee's creator was playing a role. She took advantage of people's desire to help others. Internet hoaxers often play on emotions like sympathy, fear, and greed. They use the same tricks that hoaxers have used for ages. Like inventor John W. Keely, they awe the public with technical terms. Like P. T. Barnum, they cite experts in support of their claims. Unlike those earlier schemers, they never have to come face-to-face with the people they're trying to fool.

How can you spot an Internet hoax? You can check out suspicious information on Web sites that track Internet hoaxes. (You'll find several such sites listed at the back of this book.) Be wary of any message that asks you to forward it to everyone you know. It's natural to

want to pass on virus warnings, but real virus warnings are usually announced in the press, not through e-mail. If you get an e-mail that might be a hoax, don't send it on. Don't give the hoaxer a chance to say "fooled you!"

Of course, really good hoaxes can be hard to resist. They are so much more fun than the truth. It's exciting to think that there are fairies in the garden, mysterious ape-men in the woods, or aliens in the wheat field. Just keep in mind that when something sounds too weird or too good to be true—like a mutant cat or a free trip to Disneyland—it's probably *not* true.

Find Out More

Books

Randi, James. *An Encyclopedia of Claims, Frauds, and Hoaxes of the Occult and Supernatural: Decidedly Skeptical Definitions of Alternate Realities.* New York: St. Martin's Griffin, 1997.

Sifakis, Carl. *The Big Book of Hoaxes: True Tales of the Greatest Lies Ever Told.* New York: DC Comics, 1996.

Stein, Gordon, ed. *Encyclopedia of Hoaxes.* Detroit: Gale Research, 1993.

Stein, Gordon, and Marie J. MacNee. *Scams, Shams, and Flimflams: From King Tut to Elvis Lives.* Detroit: U*X*L, 1994.

Stewart, Gail. *Famous Hoaxes.* New York: Crestwood House, 1990.

Streissguth, Thomas. *Hoaxers & Hustlers.* Minneapolis: Oliver Press, 1994.

Web sites

These sites track Internet hoaxes:

    www.urbanlegends.about.com

    www.snopes.com

    www.truthorfiction.com

    http://hoaxbusters.ciac.org

        (this U.S. Department of Energy site also has tips for detecting and dealing with false e-mails)

These sites have information on other hoaxes:

    www.circlemakers.org

        (all about crop circles, including how to make one)

    www.historybuff.com/library/refhoaxes.html

        (articles on great newspaper hoaxes, including Poe's balloon hoax)

    www.lostmuseum.cuny.edu

        (P. T. Barnum's American Museum)

    www.museumofhoaxes.com

        (extensive collection of famous hoaxes)

    www.SkepDic.com/tifraud.html

        (The Skeptic's Dictionary site includes articles about the Cardiff Giant, Bigfoot, crop circles, and more)